Disney
Winnie the Pooh

It's Fun to Learn

Where Is Your Home?

Bounce! Roo hopped as high as he could for his first bounce of the day. "That was even higher than yesterday!" Roo cheered. As he landed, he saw a little face peeking out at him.

Roo tiptoed over to the bushes. "Hi, there!" he said.

A little animal backed away from him.

"Hi, little guy. I've never seen you before," said Roo. "Are you lost?"

The animal stopped and looked up at Roo.

Then Roo saw that the animal had been chewing on the tree nearby.

"You must be really hungry," said Roo.

"Roo!" Kanga called. "Time for breakfast, dear."

"Come on," Roo said. "You can come home with me. My mama always makes lots for breakfast."

Roo's new little friend followed him back to the house.

"Why, who's this?" asked Kanga.

"I don't know, but I think he's lost!" Roo hopped into his chair. "Can he stay for breakfast?"

"Of course, dear," Kanga replied. She watched as Roo's friend began chewing on the leg of one of her chairs.

"Afterwards, we'll have to help him find his way home."

"Can't he stay with us, Mama?" asked Roo. "Please?"

"I'm afraid not, dear," Kanga replied, giving Roo's new friend a branch to chew. "His family probably misses him—just the way I'd miss you if you were lost."

Roo's little friend finished munching on his branch. For a second helping, he started chewing on the table leg.

Kanga gently stopped him. "He seems to like chewing things," said Kanga. "Maybe that's our first clue as to where he belongs."

"He must belong someplace where there's lots of wood to chew on!" cried Roo. "Which could be almost anywhere in the Hundred-Acre Wood," Kanga said to herself with a sigh.

"We'll ask Gopher to help," Roo suggested. "He's got big teeth just like Baby Munch!"

"Baby Munch?" asked Kanga.

"Just a nickname 'cause he munches everything he sees," Roo giggled as they hurried toward Gopher's hole.

"Well, ssssonny," said Gopher, "he does have a fine set of choppers. But he's not part of my family. We gophers sssstay underground in our burrows. And with that tail and those webbed feet, he seems like he might be more of a s-s-swimmer than a digger."

"Hmm . . . a swimmer," said Kanga. "Roo, dear, perhaps Baby Munch lives in a house near water, where he can swim."

"I know, I know!" Roo hopped up and down. "The lake! Come on, Baby Munch! I'll race you!"

When Kanga caught up to Roo and Baby Munch, they were sitting under a tree, talking to Pooh. "What are you doing here?" asked Kanga.

"I just stopped to show Baby Munch where bees live," said Roo. Then he turned to his new friend. "You wouldn't like it in a beehive. It's too sticky."

Baby Munch started chewing on a nearby tree. "Maybe that tree is where Baby Munch belongs!" cried Roo.

"I don't think so, dear," said Kanga.

Before Pooh ran off with his honey, he and Roo sang a simple rhyme:

Hives are where the bees go buzz, buzz, buzz all day!

I like to fill my honey pot and then be on my way!

Roo and Kanga continued their search for Baby Munch's home. Just past some thick bushes, Roo stopped suddenly. "Look!" he whispered. "Do you think this is where he belongs?"

A mama deer and her fawn were resting in their home in the thicket.

"No, maybe not," Roo said. "They look different."

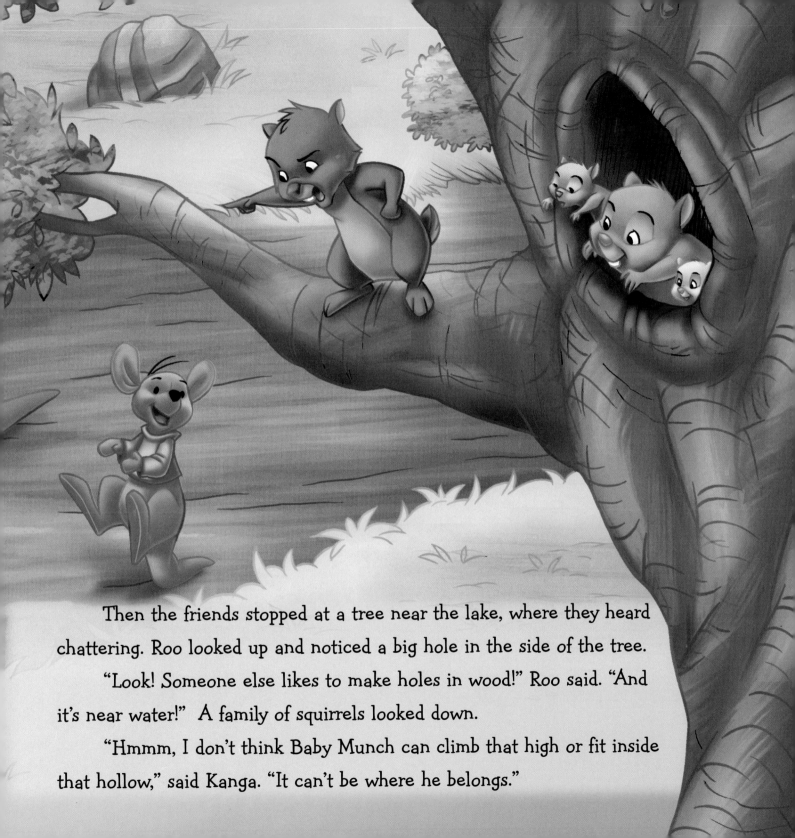

Then the friends stopped at a tree near the lake, where they heard chattering. Roo looked up and noticed a big hole in the side of the tree.

"Look! Someone else likes to make holes in wood!" Roo said. "And it's near water!" A family of squirrels looked down.

"Hmmm, I don't think Baby Munch can climb that high or fit inside that hollow," said Kanga. "It can't be where he belongs."

Just then Tigger bounced up to Roo. "What's all the chatter, Buddy Boy?" he asked.
"Well," Roo began, "the squirrels are mad because Baby Munch tried to eat their home."
"Hoo-hoo-hoo!" laughed Tigger. "I wonder what the little guy will have for dessert!"

Suddenly a twig fell from the tree above them. Baby Munch caught it and chewed it up happily. A mother bird chirped from the tree where she was building a nest.

"Hey, lookee there!" cried Tigger. "This bird's using twigs 'n stuff like Baby Munch."

"Hmmm," said Roo. "That's true, but Baby Munch doesn't have wings, and he seems too big to fit in that home. It can't be where he belongs."

Tigger joined Roo and Kanga as they hurried Baby Munch away from the tree. Suddenly, Baby Munch took off running. He must have known what was beyond the trees—it was a stream!

"Look, Mama!" cried Roo. "Water!"

Quack, quack, quack! A mother duck hurried her ducklings out of their lakeside nest. Maybe that was where Baby Munch belonged.

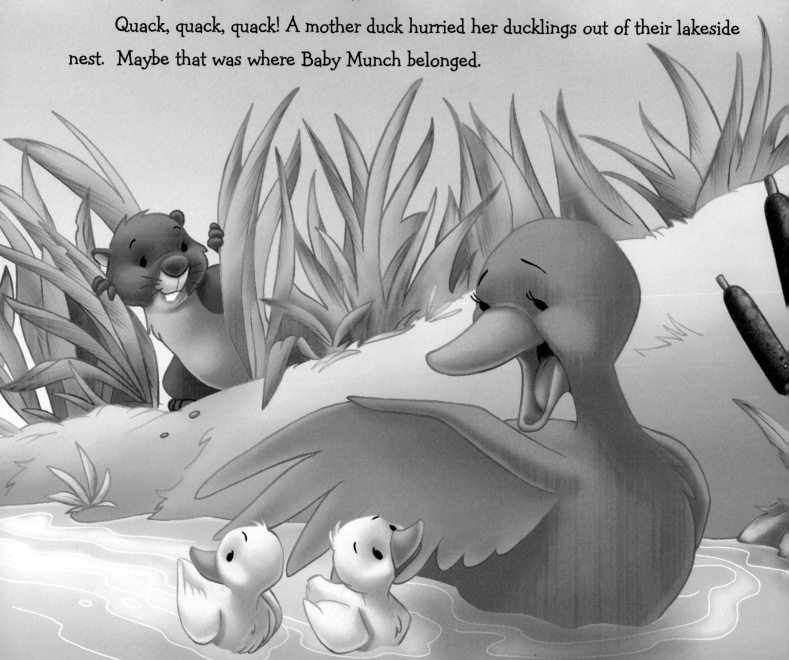

"I think she wants us to stay away from her nest," said Tigger.

"Then it can't be Baby Munch's mama," said Roo.

"You got that right, Roo Boy!" Tigger agreed. "Mrs. Kanga always hugs ya. I've never seen her run away from you."

Kanga was getting worried. They still hadn't seen Baby Munch's family or home.

Roo sank down on the bank near a pile of muddy sticks. "Poor Baby Munch! How are we ever going to find his home?"

Baby Munch slapped his tail on the ground as if he were asking the same question.

Just then a wet face popped up out of the water near the pile of muddy sticks. This little face had big teeth that held a long stick and looked just like Baby Munch.

"Hey, lookee here!" said Tigger. "Now, that looks like somebuddy who belongs to Baby Munch!"

"Where, where?" said Roo. "I don't see it."

Suddenly the animal started swimming toward Baby Munch! Baby Munch dove into the water and swam quickly to meet her.

"That must be his mama!" shouted Roo. "They look like each other—the way we do, Mama!"

"There, Roo," said Kanga. "Baby Munch has found his home at last!"

Just then Owl flew overhead. "I say now, Roo. I see you've made a new beaver friend."

"Beaver?" asked Roo. "Is that what he is?"

"Yes-yes-yes," said Owl confidently. "A beaver, indeed."

"See ya later, Baby Munch," shouted Roo as he, Tigger, and Kanga waved good-bye. "Say, Mama, do you think I can visit him sometime?"

"Of course, dear," said Kanga, "but let's make sure neither one of you wanders so far away from home that anyone gets lost again."

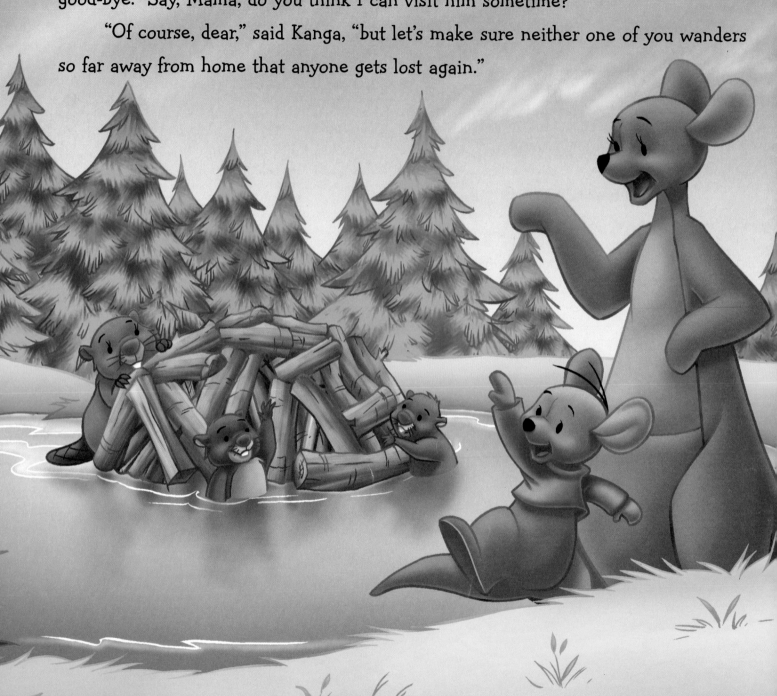

"Yup-eroo!" said Tigger. "There's no place like home, sweet home."

"Where you belong!" added Roo.

Roo made up a little rhyme. "Listen, Mama," he said:

I can't live underwater; I can't live in a tree.

I can't live in a hole; a house is home for me!

Fun to Learn Activity

Wasn't Baby Munch cute? I'm so glad we found his home by the lake. Can you describe the different homes for the animals and birds that we saw along the way?

Look around your neighborhood for different kinds of animals and birds. Then see if you can find their homes! How are they different from your house?